VEGETARIAN COOKING

Designed by Sally Strugnell and Claire Leighton
Illustrations by Christine Berrington
Food photography by Peter Barry
Edited by Ros Cocks, Jillian Stewart and Laura Potts

CLB 3278

This 1993 edition published by Magna Books, Magna Road, Wigston, Leicester LE18 4ZH.

Printed and bound in Singapore.
ISBN 1 85422 501 4

VEGETARIAN COOKING

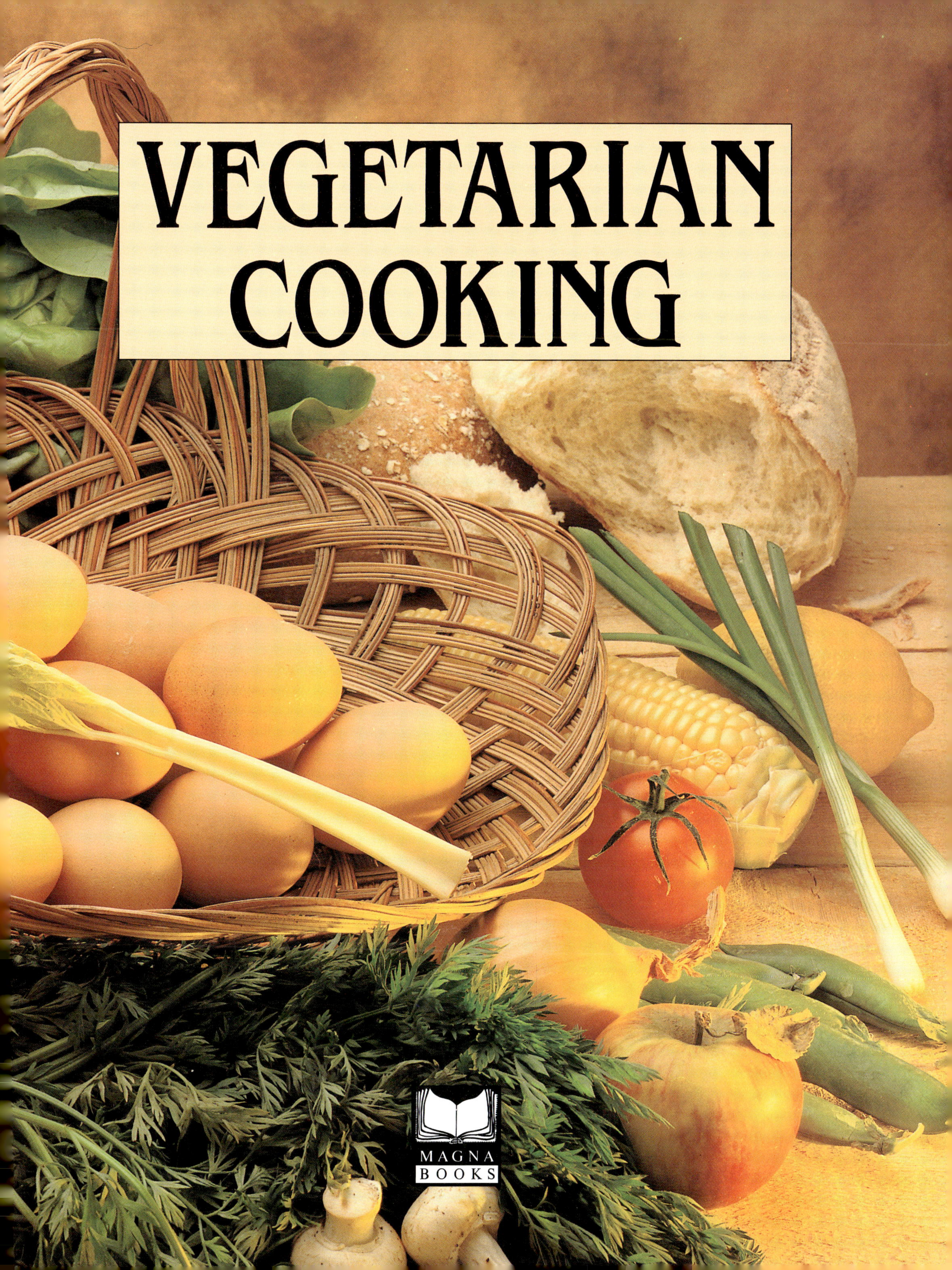

MAGNA BOOKS

INTRODUCTION

Vegetarianism is on the increase. We are frequently inundated with media reports advising us to cut down on high cholesterol foods, especially red meat. Consequently, many people feel that if they embrace a vegetarian diet, they are contributing to their own good health – as it is acknowledged that vegetarians generally have less heart disease, less intestinal disorders and better teeth. Environmental and moral arguments about intensive farming and the use of land to feed livestock also feature strongly in the argument for vegetarianism, and have convinced many people to change their eating habits.

Preparing interesting vegetarian meals is not as difficult as it would have been only a dozen years ago. The market has responded handsomely to the trend towards vegetarianism. Our supermarkets are bursting at the seams with excellent quality fruit and vegetables from all over the world. The choice of dairy products has also increased dramatically over the past decades, with great emphasis being given to varieties of yogurt and cheese. Supermarkets and healthfood shops store an array of grains such as flours, rices, couscous, bulgar, and oats; pulses such as lentils, kidney beans, haricot beans, and chick peas; and soya bean derivatives such as bean curd, smoked bean curd, and soya milk. The choice of vegetarian foods has never been greater nor the variety more stimulating. For many people vegetarian cooking has become an exciting creative pastime as well as the basis for a whole new way of eating.

Whether you are embarking on a vegetarian diet, or simply preparing a few vegetarian meals every week, it is important to have some grasp of your nutritional requirements. As with any diet, the less refined or processed the ingredients the better. Pulses and nuts are a good stand-by in the larder, but they do deteriorate with time, and notice should be taken of the 'use by' date. Fruit and vegetables are best eaten as fresh as possible. Dairy products should be kept in the refrigerator, and also eaten by the 'use by' date. There is a danger of vegetarians over-doing the cheese. This can result in a diet high in saturated fats. Dairy products are not the only decent source of protein left to the non-meat eater – pulses and nuts are a perfectly adequate source. If you are strict vegetarian you must ensure the correct food groups are combined to provide an adequate protein supply. Typical complementary pairs include: beans and grains – i.e. serve a lentil dish with rice; nuts and vegetables – nuts go well with green vegetables such as spinach; cheese and vegetables – top a vegetable casserole with melted cheese; fruit and yogurt – whether whipped together or served separately.

There is something for everyone and every season included in these pages. You will find tempting party dips and pates, and some really unusual starters, salads and soups, the latter often teaming up surprising partners with perfect success, such as fennel and watercress, and spinach and apple. The main course dishes comprise of pies, curries, casseroles and some very satisfying vegetarian equivalents of popular continental meat dishes, such as moussaka and lasagne. The desserts are not indulgent extravaganzas, but interesting fruity puddings appropriate for a book that is concerned with the feeling of good health that comes from vegetarian cooking.

PRESCRIPTIONS
Tele-rents
Holland
12/120

Easy Lentil Soup

Preparation Time: 10 minutes **Cooking Time:** 15-20 minutes **Serves:** 4-6

A good old-fashioned soup which is sure to please all the family.

Ingredients
225g/8oz split red lentils
2 tbsps butter or margarine
1 medium onion, finely chopped
2 stalks celery, finely diced
2 carrots, finely diced
Grated rind of 1 lemon
1150ml/2 pints light vegetable stock
Salt and pepper

Pick over the lentils and remove any stones. Rinse well.

Heat the butter or margarine in a pan and sauté the onion for 2-3 minutes. Add the diced celery and carrots and let the vegetables sweat for 5-10 minutes. Stir in the lentils, add the lemon rind, stock and salt and pepper to taste. Bring to the boil, reduce the heat and simmer for 15-20 minutes until the vegetables are tender.

Roughly blend the soup in a liquidizer, it should not be too smooth. Check the seasoning and reheat gently.

Watercress and Mushroom Pâté

Preparation Time: 10 minutes **Cooking Time:** 5 minutes **Serves:** 4

A delightful pâté which is perfect garnished with lime or lemon wedges and served with thinly sliced brown bread and butter.

Ingredients

2 tbsps butter
1 medium onion, finely chopped
90g/3oz dark, flat mushrooms, finely chopped
1 bunch watercress, finely chopped
120g/4oz low fat curd cheese
Few drops shoyu sauce (Japanese soy sauce)
Scant ½ tsp caraway seeds
Black pepper

Melt the butter over a low heat and cook the onion until soft but not coloured. Raise the heat, add the mushrooms and cook quickly for 2 minutes. Put in the chopped watercress and stir for about 30 seconds until it becomes limp.

Place the contents of the pan in a liquidizer together with the cheese and shoyu sauce. Blend until smooth. Stir in the caraway seeds and pepper to taste.

Put into individual ramekin dishes or one large serving dish and chill for at least 2 hours until firm.

Savoury Tomatoes

Preparation Time: 10 minutes **Serves:** 4

An ideal vegetarian starter for slimmers.

Ingredients
4 large Spanish tomatoes
60ml/4 tbsps cottage cheese
1 tsp ground cumin
1 green pepper, de-seeded and diced
Salt and pepper
4 tbsps pumpkin seeds
1 bunch watercress

Slice off the tops of the tomatoes. Remove the seeds and leave upside down to drain.

Rub the cottage cheese through a sieve to achieve a smooth consistency, add a little milk if necessary. Stir in the cumin, pepper and seasoning. Divide the mixture into four and stuff the tomatoes.

Dry roast the pumpkin seeds in a frying pan until they are lightly browned. Sprinkle over the tomatoes. Chill until required. Serve on a bed of watercress.

Spinach and Apple Soup

Preparation Time: 15 minutes **Cooking Time:** 15 minutes **Serves:** 4

The two main flavours complement each other perfectly in this hearty soup.

Ingredients

2 tbsps butter or margarine
1 small onion, chopped
2 tbsps wholemeal flour
570ml/1 pint vegetable stock
450g/1lb spinach, shredded
225g/8oz apple purée
280ml/½ pint milk
Salt and pepper
Pinch of nutmeg
Lemon juice
Natural yogurt
A little parsley, finely chopped

Melt the butter in a large saucepan and fry the onion until soft. Add the flour and cook to a roux. Add the stock slowly, stir well and simmer for 10 minutes. Add the spinach and cook until tender. Cool slightly and mix in the apple purée. Place all the ingredients in a liquidizer and blend until smooth.

Return to the pan and reheat slowly together with the milk. Add the salt, pepper, nutmeg and lemon juice to taste. Serve in individual bowls with the yogurt swirled on the top and garnished with chopped parsley.

Mushrooms and Tofu in Garlic Butter

Preparation Time: 10 minutes **Cooking Time:** 12 minutes **Serves:** 4

A quick and delicious vegetarian starter.

Ingredients
225g/8oz button mushrooms
2.5cm/1 inch root ginger
225g/8oz smoked tofu
120g/4oz butter
4 small clove garlic, crushed
2 tbsps chopped parsley

Wipe the mushrooms with a damp cloth. Peel and grate the root ginger. Cut the smoked tofu into 1.25cm/½-inch squares.

Melt the butter in a frying pan. Add the crushed garlic and ginger and fry gently for 2 minutes. Add the mushrooms and cook gently for 4-5 minutes until the mushrooms are softened. Finally, add the smoked tofu and heat through.

Divide between 4 individually heated dishes, sprinkle with chopped parsley and serve at once.

Fennel and Walnut Soup

Preparation Time: about 15 minutes **Cooking Time:** 45-50 minutes
Serves: 4

The delicious and unusual combination of flavours makes this soup perfect for special occasions.

Ingredients

1 bulb fennel, chopped
1 head celery, chopped
1 large onion, chopped
1 tbsp olive or sunflower oil
90g/3oz walnuts, crushed
1150ml/2 pints vegetable stock, bean stock or water
3 tbsps Pernod
140ml/¼ pint single cream
Salt and pepper
Parsley to garnish

Sauté the fennel, celery and onion in the oil over a low heat. Add the walnuts and stock and simmer for half an hour. Liquidize the simmered ingredients together and return to the pan.

Add the Pernod, single cream and salt and pepper. Reheat gently without boiling and serve garnished with parsley.

Hummus

Preparation Time: 10 minutes **Standing Time:** 1 hour **Serves:** 4

A classic starter which also makes the perfect vegetarian snack.

Ingredients

225g/8oz cooked chick peas (reserve stock)
60ml/4 tbsps light tahini
Juice of 2 lemons
90ml/6 tbsps olive oil
3-4 cloves garlic, crushed
Salt

Put the cooked chick peas into a liquidizer together with 140ml/¼ pint of the reserved stock. Add the tahini, lemon juice, half of the olive oil, the garlic, and salt to taste. Liquidize until smooth, adding a little more stock if it is too thick.

Leave to stand for an hour or so to let the flavours develop. Serve on individual dishes with the remaining olive oil drizzled over the top.

Mushroom Stroganoff

Preparation Time: 10 minutes **Cooking Time:** 20 minutes **Serves:** 4-6

A great favourite which is much appreciated by all age groups.

Ingredients

2 medium onions, sliced
5 sticks celery, chopped
50g/2oz butter or margarine
450g/1lb tiny button mushrooms
½ tsp mixed herbs
½ tsp basil
1 heaped tbsp unbleached flour
280ml/½ pint stock
Salt and pepper
60ml/4 tbsps sour cream or yogurt
Chopped parsley

Put the onions and celery into a large pan together with the butter or margarine and sauté over a low heat until the onions are transparent. Add the mushrooms and cook for 2-3 minutes until the juices run. Add the mixed herbs and basil. Stir in the flour and cook for 1 minute. Add the stock and seasoning and allow to cook gently for 8-10 minutes.

Remove from the heat, stir in the soured cream and adjust the seasoning if necessary. Heat very gently to serving temperature but do not allow to boil. Garnish with the chopped parsley and serve at once.

Lentil Moussaka

Preparation Time: 45 minutes **Cooking Time:** 1 hour 10 minutes **Serves:** 4-6

Try a taste of the Greek Islands with this classic dish.

Ingredients

150g/5oz green lentils
1 large aubergine, sliced
4-5 tbsps oil
1 large onion, chopped
1 clove garlic, crushed
1 large carrot, diced
4 sticks celery, finely chopped
1-2 tsps mixed herbs
1 × 400g/14oz tin tomatoes
1 tbsp shoyu sauce (Japanese soy sauce)
Black pepper
2 medium potatoes, cooked and sliced
2 large tomatoes, sliced

Sauce

60g/2oz margarine
2 tbsps brown rice flour
430ml/¾ pint milk
1 large egg, separated
2 tbsps grated Cheddar cheese
1 tsp nutmeg

Cook the lentils in plenty of water until soft. Drain and reserve the liquid. Fry the aubergine in the oil, drain well and set aside. Sauté the onion, garlic, carrot, celery and a little of the lentil stock. Simmer with the lid on until just tender. Add the lentils, mixed herbs and tinned tomatoes. Simmer gently for 3-4 minutes. Season with the shoyu and pepper.

Place a layer of the lentil mixture in a large casserole dish and cover with half of the aubergine slices. Cover the aubergine slices with half of the potato slices and all the tomato. Repeat with the remaining lentils, aubergines and potatoes.

To make the sauce, melt the margarine in a saucepan, remove from the heat and stir in the flour to make a roux. Add the milk gradually, blending well, so that the sauce is smooth and lump free. Return to the heat and stir continually until the sauce thickens. Remove the pan from the heat and cool slightly. Add the egg yolk, stir in the cheese and add the nutmeg. Beat the egg white until it is stiff, then carefully fold into the sauce. Pour the sauce over the moussaka, covering the dish completely. Bake at 180°C/350°F/Gas Mark 4 for about 40 minutes until the top is golden brown and puffy.

Lollo Rosso Salad

Preparation Time: 10 minutes **Serves:** 4

A colourful variation of a Greek Salad.

Ingredients

½ lollo rosso lettuce
3 medium tomatoes, diced
1 red pepper, chopped
1 green pepper, chopped
3 sticks celery, diced
⅓ cucumber, diced
200g/7oz Cheshire cheese, cubed
16 black olives

Dressing

1 tbsp tarragon vinegar
3 tbsps olive oil

Wash the lettuce and dry it well. Break into pieces with your fingers and put it into a large bowl. Add the tomatoes, pepper, celery, cucumber and cheese. Mix together the vinegar and olive oil, and pour over the salad. Mix gently. Divide the salad between 4 individual dishes and place 4 olives on the top of each one.

Potato Nests

Preparation Time: 10 minutes **Cooking Time:** 25-30 minutes **Serves:** 2

This supper dish is an excellent way of using up leftover cooked potatoes.

Ingredients

1 onion, finely chopped
450g/1lb potatoes, cooked in their skins
A little milk
Knob of butter
Salt and pepper
2 eggs
2 tbsps grated cheese

Cook the onion in a little water until softened. Drain. Peel the cooked potatoes and mash them with the milk, butter and seasoning. Add the drained onion and mix well.

Divide the mixture into two and make 'nests' on a greased baking sheet. Crack an egg into each nest and sprinkle with grated cheese. Bake at 200°C/400°F/Gas Mark 6 for 20-25 minutes or until the eggs are set.

Indian Vegetable Curry

Preparation Time: 30 minutes **Cooking Time:** 1 hour 30 minutes **Serves:** 4

A wonderfully tasty curry which has the added advantage of freezing well.

Ingredients
Spices
2 tsps turmeric
1 tsp cumin
1 tsp mustard seed
1 tsp fenugreek
4 tsps coriander
½ tsp chilli powder
1 tsp ginger
1 tsp black peppercorns

1lb onions, finely chopped
Ghee or vegetable oil (vary amount to suit – about 60ml/4 tbsps)
280ml/½ pint sterilised milk
2 tbsps white wine vinegar
1 × 400g/14oz tin tomatoes, liquidized with their juice
1 tbsp tomato purée
2 tsps brown sugar
1 stock cube dissolved in little boiling water
900g/2lbs chopped mushrooms or mixed vegetables (e.g. mushrooms, cauliflower, carrots, potatoes, okra)

Grind all the spices together, this amount will make 3 tbsps of curry powder. Fry the onions in the ghee or vegetable oil until golden. Add the ground spices, lower the heat and cook for 3 minutes, stirring all the time. Add the milk and vinegar and stir well. Add the liquidized tomatoes, tomato purée, sugar and stock. Bring to the boil, cover and simmer very gently for 1 hour.

Add the vegetables and cook until tender – about 30 minutes.

Spinach, Corn and Nut Raised Pie

Preparation Time: 40 minutes **Cooking Time:** 1 hour 15 minutes **Serves:** 6

An attractive pie which is suitable for family meals and entertaining.

Ingredients
450g/1lb spinach
1 onion, chopped
2 tbsps oil
120g/4oz hazelnuts, finely chopped
120g/4oz brazil nuts, finely chopped
120g/4oz wholemeal breadcrumbs
120g/4oz sweetcorn
1 tsp oregano
½ tsp sage
1 tbsp freshly chopped parsley
1 tsp shoyu (Japanese soy sauce)
2 tbsps tahini
280ml/½ pint stock
Salt and pepper

Pastry
340g/12oz wholemeal flour
1 tsp baking powder
120g/4oz vegetable fat
175ml/6fl oz water
Pinch of salt

Steam the spinach until soft. Drain well and chop finely. Fry the onion in the oil until soft.

Mix together all the dry ingredients, add the spinach and onion, add the shoyu, tahini and sufficient stock to give a moist texture. Season to taste.

For the pastry, mix together the dry ingredients. Melt the fat in the water and heat until about to boil. Add the liquid to the flour and mix well. Add extra boiling water if the mixture is too dry. Put two thirds of the dough into a 17.8cm/7″ pie tin and push into shape. Put the filling into the pie case and press down well. Roll out the remaining dough and make a pie lid. Glaze the top and make two small steam holes. Bake at 225°C/425°F/Gas Mark 7 for 20 minutes, reduce the heat to 190°C/375°F/Gas Mark 5 for a further 50 minutes or until golden brown.

Oven Baked Spaghetti

Preparation Time: 10 minutes **Cooking Time:** 20-25 minutes **Serves:** 4

A convenient way to cook this favourite mid-week meal.

Ingredients

225g/8oz wholewheat spaghetti, cooked
2 × 400g/14oz tins tomatoes, roughly chopped
1 large onion, grated
1 tsp oregano
Salt and pepper
120g/4oz Cheddar cheese
2 tbsps Parmesan cheese, grated

Grease four individual ovenproof dishes and place a quarter of the spaghetti in each one. Pour the tomatoes over the top. Add the onion, sprinkle with oregano and season well. Slice the cheese finely and arrange over the top of the spaghetti mixture. Sprinkle with Parmesan and bake at 180°C/350°F/ Gas Mark 4 for 30 minutes.

Tabouleh

Preparation Time: 20 minutes **Standing Time:** 2 hours **Serves:** 6

This is a traditional salad from the Middle East. The main ingredient is bulgar which is partially cooked cracked wheat and only needs soaking for a short while before it is ready to eat.

Ingredients
180-200g/6-7oz bulgar wheat
1 tsp salt
350ml/12fl oz boiling water
450g/1lb tomatoes, chopped
½ cucumber, diced
3-4 spring onions

Dressing
3 tbsps olive oil
3 tbsps lemon juice
2 tbsps fresh mint
4 tbsps fresh parsley
2 cloves garlic, crushed

Mix the bulgar wheat with the salt, pour over the boiling water and leave for 15-20 minutes. All the water will then be absorbed. Mix together the ingredients for the dressing and pour over the soaked bulgar. Fold in lightly with a spoon. Leave for two hours or overnight in a fridge or cool place.

Add the salad ingredients and serve.

Butter Beans in Tomato Sauce

Preparation Time: 20 minutes **Cooking Time:** 1½-1¾ hours **Serves:** 4-6

A tasty tomato sauce perfectly complements the beans in this easy recipe.

Ingredients

180g/6oz butter beans, soaked overnight
1 onion, sliced
2 tbsps vegetable oil
6 medium tomatoes, sliced
1 bay leaf
2 tbsps flour
A little milk
Salt and pepper
Chopped parsley

Drain the butter beans and put into a pan with fresh water to cover, cook slowly until soft. Cook the onions in the oil with the tomatoes and bay leaf until soft. Stir in the flour, and add a little cooking water from the beans to make a thick sauce. Stir well and add a little milk and seasoning to taste. Remove the bay leaf and pour the sauce over the beans. Sprinkle with chopped parsley and serve.

Lentil Savoury

Preparation Time: 15 minutes **Cooking Time:** 35-45 minutes **Serves:** 4

This dish is quick and easy to prepare and very nutritious.

Ingredients

180g/6oz lentils
½ tsp basil
½ tsp mixed herbs
2 medium onions, chopped
50g/2oz margarine
2 tbsps tomato purée
1 × 400g/14oz tin tomatoes
1 tsp brown sugar
Salt and pepper
180g/6oz sliced Cheddar cheese
140ml/¼ pint soured cream

Pick over the lentils and wash thoroughly. Place in a large, thick-bottomed pan, cover with water and bring to the boil. Add the herbs and simmer with the lentils until tender – about 25 minutes depending on the age of the lentils.

Sauté the onion in the fat until soft. Add the lentils and all the other ingredients apart from cheese and cream. Simmer for 15 minutes until thickened and pour into a greased ovenproof dish. Cover with the cheese and cream and grill or bake at 180°C/375°F/Gas Mark 4 until the cheese has melted.

Asparagus and Olive Quiche

Preparation Time: 20 minutes **Cooking Time:** 40 minutes
Makes: 2 × 25cm/10-inch quiches

An interesting combination which gives a new twist to a classic dish.

Ingredients

1 tbsp oil
2 onions, finely chopped
6 eggs
570ml/1 pint single cream
1 tsp salt
Pinch of nutmeg
Salt and pepper
2 tbsps flour
2 tins green asparagus tips
180g/6oz green olives
90g/3oz grated Cheddar cheese
2 × 25cm/10 inch part-baked pastry shells
2 tbsps Parmesan cheese
50g/2oz butter

Heat the oil and sauté the onions until soft. Whisk the eggs with the cream. Add the salt, nutmeg and seasoning. Mix a little of the mixture with the flour until smooth, then add to the cream mixture.

Arrange the asparagus tips, olives and onion in the pastry shells and pour the cream mixture over the top. Sprinkle with the grated Cheddar and Parmesan. Dot with butter and bake at 190°C/375°F/Gas Mark 5 for 25 minutes. Turn down the oven to 180°C/350°F/Gas Mark 4 for a further 15 minutes until the quiches are golden.

Fifteen Minute Goulash

Preparation Time: 10 minutes **Cooking Time:** 15 minutes **Serves:** 4

This quick and easy goulash is best served with baked potatoes.

Ingredients

1 onion, finely chopped
1 clove garlic, crushed
2 carrots, diced
3 medium courgettes, diced
2 tbsps olive oil
1 tbsp paprika
Pinch of nutmeg
1 heaped tbsp freshly chopped parsley
1 tbsp tomato purée
1 × 400g/14oz tin tomatoes
225g/8oz cooked red kidney beans or 1 × 400g/14oz tin, drained and washed
225g/8oz cooked white kidney beans or 1 × 400g/14oz tin, drained and washed
140ml/¼ pint tomato juice or stock
Salt and pepper
Soured cream or yogurt to serve

Put the onion, garlic, carrots and courgettes into a pan with the olive oil and sauté for 5 minutes until softened. Stir in the paprika, nutmeg, parsley and tomato purée. Add the rest of the ingredients except cream or yogurt and cook over a low heat for 10 minutes.

Turn onto a hot serving dish and top with a little soured cream or yogurt.

Pasta and Avocado Salad

Preparation Time: 10 minutes **Cooking Time:** 35 minutes **Serves:** 4

The perfect lunch or supper salad for guests.

Ingredients

225g/8oz pasta shapes
3 tbsps mayonnaise
2 tsps tahini
1 orange
½ medium red pepper, chopped
1 medium avocado
Pumpkin seeds to garnish

Cook the pasta until soft and leave to cool. Mix together the mayonnaise and tahini. Segment the orange and chop into small pieces, retain any juice. Chop the pepper. Stir the mayonnaise mixture, pepper and orange (plus juice) into the pasta. Just before serving, cube the avocado and stir in carefully. Serve on an oval dish, decorated with pumpkin seeds.

Imam Bayildi

Preparation Time: 25 minutes **Cooking Time:** 1 hour **Serves:** 4

Imam Bayildi means "the priest has fainted". Apparently this vegetarian dish was so delicious that the priest fainted with delight!

Ingredients

2 large aubergines
140ml/¼ pint olive oil
2 onions, finely chopped
2 cloves garlic, crushed
225g/8oz tomatoes, skinned and chopped
½ tsp mixed spice
Juice of ½ lemon
1 tsp brown sugar
1 tbsp chopped parsley
1 tbsp pine kernels
Salt and pepper

Halve the aubergines lengthways, and scoop out the flesh with a sharp knife leaving a substantial shell so they do not disintegrate when cooked. Sprinkle the shells with a little salt and leave upside down on a plate for 30 minutes to drain away any bitter juices.

Meanwhile, heat half the oil in a saucepan and fry the onion and garlic until just softened. Add the scooped out aubergine flesh, tomatoes, mixed spice, lemon juice, sugar, parsley, pine kernels and a little seasoning. Simmer for about 20 minutes until the mixture has thickened.

Wash and dry the aubergine shells and spoon the filling into the halves. Place side by side in a buttered ovenproof dish. Mix the remaining oil with 140ml/¼ pint water and a little seasoning. Pour around the aubergines and bake at 180°C/350°F/Gas Mark 4 for 30-40 minutes or until tender.

Savoury Grain Casserole

Preparation Time: 10 minutes **Cooking Time:** 1 hour 15 minutes **Serves:** 2-4

Serve as a complete meal for 2 people or serve accompanied with lightly steamed vegetables for 4 people.

Ingredients

90g/3oz brown rice
90g/3oz split peas
2 sticks celery, very finely chopped
1 medium onion, very finely chopped
120g/4oz mushrooms, chopped
1 × 400g/14oz tin tomatoes, drained and chopped or 225g/8oz tomatoes, peeled and chopped
½ tsp dill seeds
½ tsp thyme
2 tbsps shoyu sauce (Japanese soy sauce)
1 egg, beaten
120g/4oz Cheddar cheese, grated

Cover the rice with water and cook for 10-15 minutes and drain. Cover the split peas with water and cook for 20 minutes until just tender but not mushy and drain.

Meanwhile, combine the celery, onion, mushrooms, tomatoes, dill, thyme, shoyu and the egg in a large bowl. Stir in the rice and peas. Place the mixture in a greased ovenproof casserole dish and cook for 45 minutes at 180°C/350°F/Gas Mark 4.

Remove from the oven and sprinkle with the grated cheese. Return to the oven for 10 minutes until the cheese has melted. Serve at once.

Ratatouille Pie with Cheese and Peanut Pastry

Preparation Time: 30 minutes **Cooking Time:** 1 hour **Serves:** 4-6

A colourful dish to make in the autumn when aubergines and courgettes are cheap and plentiful.

Ingredients

Ratatouille

2 tbsps olive oil
2 onions, chopped
4 tomatoes, sliced
1 aubergine, sliced
3 courgettes, finely sliced
2 sticks celery, chopped

White sauce

60g/2oz margarine
60g/2oz flour
430ml/¾ pint milk

Pastry

60g/2oz butter
120g/4oz self raising flour
3 tbsps finely grated cheese
3 tbsps finely chopped salted peanuts
A little milk
Beaten egg

Put the oil and all the vegetables into a large pan and cook gently for about 20 minutes or until soft.

To make the sauce, melt the margarine in a separate pan, stir in the flour and cook for 2 minutes, stirring all the time. Gradually add the milk and bring to boiling point. Stir the sauce into the vegetable mixture and put into an ovenproof dish.

For the pastry rub the butter into the flour and add the cheese and peanuts. Add a little milk and roll out the pastry. Place on top of the ratatouille mixture, trim and brush with beaten egg. Bake 190°C/375°F/Gas Mark 5 for about 30 minutes or until golden brown.

Sweet Bean Curry

Preparation Time: 25 minutes **Cooking Time:** 1 hour 25 minutes **Serves:** 4

This excellent curry will freeze well for up to six weeks.

Ingredients

180g/6oz red kidney beans, soaked overnight
30g/1oz butter or margarine
1 onion, sliced
1 apple, cored and chopped
180g/6oz mushrooms, sliced
1 tbsp curry powder
1 tbsp unbleached flour
570ml/1 pint bean stock or bean stock and water
Salt
1 tbsp lemon juice
1 tbsp chutney
2 tbsps sultanas
60g/2oz coconut cream, grated or chopped

Drain the beans, put into a large pan and cover with cold water. Bring to the boil and boil vigorously for 10-15 minutes, turn down the heat and boil for about an hour until the beans are tender but still whole.

Melt the butter or margarine and cook the onion until it is very brown. Add the apple and mushrooms and cook for 2-3 minutes. Add the curry powder and flour and cook for a couple of minutes, stirring all the time. Gradually add the bean stock and stir until smooth. Add the seasoning, lemon juice, chutney, sultanas and beans and cook for 10-15 minutes. Just before serving add the coconut cream and stir until dissolved.

Broccoli and Cauliflower Salad

Preparation Time: 10 minutes **Serves:** 4

Serve this simple salad with crackers.

Ingredients
1 red pepper
340g/12oz broccoli
340g/12oz cauliflower
1 tbsp roasted almond flakes

Dressing
4 tbsps Greek yogurt
2 tbsps lemon juice
2 tbsps olive oil
Salt and pepper
Pinch of nutmeg

De-seed the pepper and cut into matchstick pieces. Wash and trim the broccoli and cauliflower and break into small florets. Place the pepper, broccoli and cauliflower in a mixing bowl. Combine the yogurt, lemon juice, olive oil, seasoning and nutmeg in a screw top jar and shake well. Spoon the dressing over the salad and mix together well. Divide the mixture between 4 individual serving plates and garnish with the almond flakes.

P
S

Beany Lasagne

Preparation Time: 20 minutes **Cooking Time:** 60 minutes **Serves:** 4-6

This tasty lasagne is suitable for a family meal or entertaining friends.

Ingredients
8 strips wholewheat lasagne
1 large onion, finely chopped
1 tbsp vegetable oil
1-2 cloves garlic, crushed
225g/8oz cooked aduki beans
1 green pepper, de-seeded and chopped
1 × 400g/14oz can chopped tomatoes
1 tbsp tomato purée
1 tsp dried basil
1 tsp dried oregano
Shoyu sauce (Japanese soy sauce) or salt
Pepper

Sauce
30g/1oz margarine or butter
1 tbsp plain wholewheat flour
430ml/¾ pint dairy or soya milk
2 tbsps grated Cheddar cheese (optional)
Salt and pepper

Cook the lasagne in a large pan of boiling, salted water for 8-10 minutes until "al dente". Drain well and drape over a cooling rack or the sides of a colander to cool and prevent sticking together.

Soften the onion in a little oil, sprinkling with a little salt to draw out the juice. Add the crushed garlic. Add the beans, green pepper, chopped tomatoes, tomato purée and herbs. Simmer for about 10 minutes or until the vegetables are tender. Add shoyu sauce and season to taste.

To make the sauce, combine the margarine, flour and cold milk. Gradually bring to the boil, stirring continuously. When thickened, allow to simmer, partly covered, for approximately 6 minutes. Stir the cheese into the sauce and season.

Layer the lasagne in a greased dish in the following order: half the bean mix, half the pasta, rest of the bean mix, rest of the pasta, and top with the cheese sauce. Bake at 180°C/350°F/Gas Mark 4 for 35 minutes or until golden brown and bubbling. Serve in the dish in which it has been cooked.

Green Lentils with Fresh Ginger and Spices

Preparation Time: 25 minutes **Cooking Time:** 45 minutes **Serves:** 4

There's certainly no lack of taste in this spicy lentil mix.

Ingredients

180g/6oz green or Continental lentils
Water or stock to cover
30g/1oz margarine or 1 tbsp soya or sunflower oil
1 medium onion, finely chopped
2.5cm/1-inch piece fresh root ginger, grated or finely chopped
1 tsp garam masala
1 tsp cumin seeds
1 tsp coriander seeds, crushed
1 tsp green cardamom pods, seeds removed and crushed
1 medium carrot, diced
1 × 400g/14oz can peeled Italian tomatoes
60g/2oz mushrooms, finely chopped
1 tbsp shoyu sauce (Japanese soy sauce)
1 tbsp cider vinegar
Salt and pepper
Freshly chopped parsley or coriander to garnish

Pick over the lentils and wash thoroughly. Place in a large, thick-bottomed saucepan, cover with water or stock and bring to the boil. Turn off the heat, cover and leave to begin to swell.

Meanwhile, heat the margarine or oil in a separate saucepan and gently fry the onion, ginger and spices until they are well combined, softening and giving off a tempting aroma. Add to the lentils, bring to the boil and start to add the other vegetables, allowing several minutes between each addition, beginning with the carrot followed by the tomatoes and lastly the chopped mushrooms. Stir frequently to prevent sticking and check on liquid quantity regularly, adding more water or stock as necessary.

Just before the end of the cooking time – after approximately 25 minutes depending on the age of the lentils – add the shoyu, cider vinegar and salt and pepper. Cook for a few more minutes and serve hot garnished with slices of lemon and freshly chopped parsley or coriander.

Baked Raspberry Apples

Preparation Time: 10 minutes **Cooking Time:** 30-35 minutes **Serves:** 6

A lovely combination which is perfectly complemented by cream or yogurt.

Ingredients

2 tbsps concentrated apple juice
4 tbsps water
2 tbsps honey
1 tsp mixed spice
3 very large eating apples
225g/8oz raspberries

Put the concentrated apple juice, water, honey and mixed spice into a large bowl and mix together well. Wash the apples and, with a sharp knife, make deep zig-zag cuts around each apple. Take one half of the apple in each hand and twist gently until the two halves come apart. Remove the core and immerse each apple in the apple juice mixture. Place the apples in an ovenproof dish and bake at 200°C/400°F/Gas Mark 6 for 20-25 minutes until just soft.

Remove from the oven and top with the raspberries. Pour the remaining apple juice mixture over the raspberries and return to the oven, 150°C/300°F/Gas Mark 2 for 10 minutes. Serve at once.

Orange and Kiwi Cheesecake

Preparation Time: 15 minutes **Chilling Time:** 2 hours **Serves:** 6-8

Lemon could be used in place of orange if a tangy cheesecake is required.

Ingredients
120g/4oz margarine
225g/8oz crushed wholemeal digestive biscuits

Topping
450g/1lb Quark or skimmed milk soft cheese
120g/4oz margarine
1 medium egg, beaten
Fruit and zest of 1 orange, chopped
1 tbsp ground almonds
¼ tsp almond essence
2 kiwi fruit

Make the base by melting the margarine and adding to the biscuit crumbs. Mix well and press into a dish or flan base. Chill thoroughly.

Mix together the cheese, margarine, egg, chopped orange and zest, almonds, almond essence and one kiwi fruit, peeled and chopped.

Spread over the chilled base. Peel and slice the other kiwi-fruit and decorate the top of the cheesecake. Chill for 2 hours.

Hot Apple Pizza

Preparation Time: 45 minutes **Cooking Time:** 15-20 minutes. **Serves:** 4-6

A delicious dessert – perfect with yogurt or cream.

Ingredients
13g/½oz fresh yeast
60ml/4 tbsps warm water, hand hot
90g/3oz strong wholemeal flour
50g/2oz strong white flour
½ tsp ground cinnamon
13g/½oz butter or margarine
½ tbsp concentrated apple juice

Topping
2 red skinned dessert apples
1 tbsp raisins
1 tbsp hazelnuts
1 tbsp concentrated apple juice
13g/½oz butter or margarine

Cream the yeast with the water, add 1 teaspoon of flour and leave in a warm place for 10-15 minutes until frothy. Mix together the flours and cinnamon. Rub in the butter. Add the yeast mixture and concentrated apple juice to the flour. Mix to a stiff dough, adding more warm water if necessary. Knead well. Roll the dough into a circle, about 22.5cm/9 inches in diameter. Cover with cling film and leave to rise for 10-15 minutes.

Slice the apples evenly and arrange over the base. Sprinkle the raisins, hazelnuts and concentrated apple juice over the apples and dot with the butter or margarine. Bake on the middle shelf of the oven at 200°C/400°F/Gas Mark 6 for 15-20 minutes.

Appetisers and Soups:
Easy Lentil Soup 10
Fennel and Walnut Soup 20
Hummus 22
Mushrooms and Tofu in Garlic Butter 18
Savoury Tomatoes 14
Spinach and Apple Soup 16
Watercress and Mushroom Paté 12
Asparagus and Olive Quiche 44
Baked Raspberry Apples 64
Beany Lasagne 60
Broccoli and Cauliflower Salad 58
Butter Beans in Tomato Sauce 40
Cakes and Desserts:
Baked Raspberry Apples 64
Hot Apple Pizza 68
Oranges and Kiwi Cheesecake 66
Casseroles:
Butter Beans in Tomato Sauce 40
Fifteen Minute Goulash 46
Mushroom Stroganoff 24
Savoury Grain Casserole 52
Curries:
Indian Vegetable Curry 32
Sweet Bean Curry 56
Easy Lentil Soup 10
Fennel and Walnut Soup 20
Fifteen Minute Goulash 46
Green Lentils with Fresh Ginger and Spices 62
Hot Apple Pizza 68
Hummus 22
Imam Bayildi 50
Indian Vegetable Curry 32
Lentil Moussaka 26
Lentil Savoury 42
Lollo Rosso Salad 28
Mushroom Stroganoff 24
Mushrooms and Tofu in Garlic Butter 18
Orange and Kiwi Cheesecake 66
Oven Baked Spaghetti 36
Pasta and Avocado Salad 48
Pies and Flans:
Asparagus and Olive Quiche 44
Ratatouille Pie with Cheese and Peanut Pastry 54
Spinach, Corn and Nut Raised Pie 34
Potato Nests 30
Ratatouille Pie with Cheese and Peanut Pastry 54
Savoury Bakes:
Beany Lasagne 60
Lentil Moussaka 26
Lentil Savoury 42
Oven Baked Spaghetti 36
Savoury Grain Casserole 52
Savoury Tomatoes 14
Salads:
Broccoli and Cauliflower Salad 58
Lollo Rosso Salad 28
Pasta and Avocado Salad 48
Tabouleh 38
Snacks:
Green Lentils with Fresh Ginger and Spices 62
Imam Bayildi 50
Potato Nests 30
Spinach and Apple Soup 16
Spinach, Corn and Nut Raised Pie 34
Sweet Bean Curry 56
Tabouleh 38
Watercress and Mushroom Paté 12